I0177584

TOPIC

What Is Worry?

SCRIPTURES

1. **Matthew 6:25** — Therefore I say to you, do not worry about your life, what you will eat or what you will drink; nor about your body, what you will put on. Is not life more than food and the body more than clothing?

2. **Isaiah 41:10** — Fear not, for I am with you; be not dismayed, for I am your God. I will strengthen you, yes, I will help you, I will uphold you with My righteous right hand.

3. **Hebrews 13:5** — ...For He Himself has said, "I will never leave you nor forsake you."

4. **Ephesians 6:10** — Finally, my brethren, be strong in the Lord and in the power of His might.

5. **Proverbs 3:5-6** — Trust in the Lord with all your heart, and lean not on your own understanding; in all your ways acknowledge Him, and He shall direct your paths.

6. **Isaiah 41:13** — For I, the Lord your God, will hold your right hand, saying to you, "Fear not, I will help you."

7. **1 John 4:4** — You are of God, little children, and have overcome them, because He who is in you is greater than he who is in the world.

8. **1 John 5:4** — For whatever is born of God overcomes the world. And this is the victory that has overcome the world — our faith.

9. **1 Peter 5:5-7** — Likewise you younger people, submit yourselves to your elders. Yes, all of you be submissive to one another, and be clothed with humility, for "God resists the proud, but gives grace to the humble." Therefore humble yourselves under the mighty hand of God, that He may exalt you in due time, casting all your care upon Him, for He cares for you.

SYNOPSIS

The five lessons in this study titled *Worry, Goodbye!* will focus on the following topics:

- What Is Worry?
- What Does Jesus Say About Worry?
- Make a New Habit, Leave Worry Behind
- 'What Is the Harm If I Just Worry a Little?'
- The Secret to Peace

The emphasis of this lesson:

You don't have to live in the grip of worry! God has given you everything you need to say goodbye to worry and walk in His peace. Worry loses its power when you cast your cares on the Lord, lean on His promises, and rely on the mighty power of the Holy Spirit within you. So rise up in faith, let go of anxiety, and receive the victory that is already yours in Christ!

Can We Live Worry-Free?

Worry creeps up on us all. It's one of those quiet, persistent temptations that most of us face regularly. And because Jesus was tempted in the same way that we are (*see* Hebrews 4:15), we know He was tempted with worry too. But Jesus told us *not* to worry. We read this in Matthew 6:25, which says, "Therefore I say to you, do not worry about your life, what you will eat or what you will drink; nor about your body, what you will put on. Is not life more than food and the body more than clothing?" If Jesus told us not to worry, then He has equipped us to do it. Can we really be free from worry? Yes, we can. We can learn to say goodbye to worry!

Worry occurs when we try to settle the problem *ourselves* rather than turning our need over to the Lord and trusting in Him. Instead of coming to Him and saying, "Lord, I need Your help. I can't do this," we're keeping our problem in our *own* hands. And as long as our need is in *our* hands, it is not in *His* hands.

God's Word reminds us that we're never alone — He is present and ready to help. A glorious truth is found in Isaiah 41:10: "Fear not, for I am with you...." Additionally, Hebrews 13:5 tells us, "...For He Himself has said,

A Note From Denise Renner

The Word of God is so powerful in our lives. It is essential that every person spend time with God and study His Word in order to stay spiritually strong in these last days.

This study guide corresponds to my *TIME With Denise Renner* TV program by the same title that can be viewed at **deniserenner.org**. My desire is that through these lessons, you find the encouragement and freedom in Christ that you need. I believe the Holy Spirit is going to speak to you through the words you read in this study tool and that as you begin to use it, you will be *propelled* into the abundant life God has planned for you. I encourage you to make the effort to receive all He has for you and all He wants to do in you — it will definitely be worth it!

Whether you have walked with the Lord a long time or have just begun to follow Him, there is so much He wants to give you from His Word. He sees where you are, and He wants to meet you there.

> **Therefore do not worry about tomorrow, for tomorrow will worry about its own things. Sufficient for the day is its own trouble.**
> **— Matthew 6:34**

Your sister and friend in Jesus Christ,

Denise Renner

Worry, Goodbye!

Copyright © 2025 by Teaching You Can Trust, LLC
1814 W. Tacoma St.
Broken Arrow, OK 74012-1406

Published by Rick Renner Ministries
www.renner.org

ISBN 13: 978-1-6675-1487-1

ISBN 13 eBook: 978-1-6675-1488-8

'I will never leave you nor forsake you.'" We do not need to fear, because God is with us.

Fear says things like, "I'm alone. I have to do this myself. Nobody cares. I can't do this." It looks at all the things that could go wrong and asks again and again in every situation, "What if?" But God's Word commands us to "fear not." Why? Because He declares, "I am with you." As a believer, not only is God *with* you — but the presence of the Holy Spirit is also *inside* you and *upon* you!

The Force of an Army Is Within Us

Coming back to Isaiah 41:10, the verse goes on to say, "…Be not dismayed, for I am your God. I will strengthen you, yes, I will help you.…" Being "dismayed" is having anxiety, sorrow, or pain in our heart. We feel we are *overtaken* by the situation and find ourselves *absolutely in anxiety* over it. But God's Word says, "Be not dismayed.… I will strengthen you." That's a promise! We can "fear not" because He is with us. We can "be not dismayed" because He will strengthen us.

The promise in Isaiah 41:10 that God will "strengthen" us was written in the Old Testament, but it is also found in the New Testament. Ephesians 6:10 says, "Finally, my brethren, be strong in the Lord and in the power of His might." The phrase "be strong" describes the power of the Holy Spirit within us. Being strong does not mean we must grit our teeth and bear the situation on our own. Rather, "be strong" means to yield to the power that's inside us by the Holy Ghost.

In Ephesians 6:10, the word "power" means *the force of an army*. When we became born again, we received the Holy Spirit, and He is inside us. Within us is His magnificent power. It's not just a little power — this is *the power of an army*! We have an army on the inside, standing against the enemy. God says in Isaiah 41:10, "I will help you." As we draw on the power that is within us by the Holy Spirit, He will help us.

God's Right Hand Upholds Us

Finally, Isaiah 41:10 goes on to declare, "…I [the Lord] will uphold you with My righteous right hand." To illustrate this concept of being upheld, Denise shared in the program a personal example from the time she visited the site where Noah's Ark is believed to rest. She said:

I had the privilege of seeing Noah's Ark in Turkey last year. Though it's a little rugged going up to the Ark, when you finally reach the site, it's magnificent! It's so huge. The measurements are just like they are in the Old Testament in Genesis, and it is definitely something to see. However, the trek was challenging. When I was climbing up to the Ark, I was leaning on my son, Paul. I had a stick in my right hand, and he had me by my left arm. And I was able, by leaning on the strength of my son, to go up that steep climb.

Imagine if I had just been proud and said, 'I can do this myself.' If I hadn't leaned on my son — who was giving me his right hand, just like God gives us His right hand — I couldn't have done it.

In this example, Denise admitted that she couldn't have made the climb on her own. If she had refused her son's help, she might have hurt herself — or might never have made it to see the Ark. Sometimes in life, we can be so determined to do things on our own that we end up hurting ourselves or never reaching our goal.

Worry often says, "I can do this myself." But humility says, "I might be able to do this, but God, I need Your help. I will quit trusting in myself and *lean* on Your right hand." That's exactly what Denise did as she climbed up that steep incline. She said, "I was leaning on the stick in my right hand, but with my left hand, I was leaning on Paul's right hand." This is the invitation that God has given us — to *not* lean upon ourselves, but to lean on Him.

In Proverbs 3:5 and 6, the Bible says, "Trust in the Lord with all your heart, and lean not on your own understanding; in all your ways acknowledge Him, and He shall direct your paths." As Christians, rather than leaning on our own understanding, we are to lean on *Him*.

Fear *Reinforces* Worry — Faith *Overcomes* It

Worry knocks on everyone's door. No matter who we are or where we come from, we've all felt its weight. At any given moment, we are either worrying, being tempted to worry, or learning to overcome it. Why? Because worry is driven by fear. That's why God so often tells us not to be afraid. In Isaiah 41:13, He promises: "For I, the Lord your God, will hold your right hand, saying to you, 'Fear not, I will help you.'"

When worry comes, it tells us, "Think about this situation a little more. What happens if it doesn't work out? *What if?*" Often, instead of walking in the peace that God purchased for us, our minds become preoccupied with so much worry that it drags us into a downward spiral of our own thoughts, which can get us into trouble.

We must bring our problems out of the arena of our mind. When we quit thinking about the problems we are facing and bring them into the arena of faith, we will crush worry — because *faith overcomes fear*. First John 5:4 says, "For whatever is born of God overcomes the world. And this is the victory that has overcome the world — our faith." You overcome this world by *your faith*! Putting your faith in the Word of God will give you the power and strength to say *no* to worrying thoughts, shutting them off so you can plant your mind on God's Word.

Trust in God, and You Will Overcome

In the program, Denise shared the testimony of a mother she knows who successfully overcame worry with faith. The woman's daughter woke up one morning, sweating all over and in great distress. So the mother took her child to the hospital, where she learned that other children in the hospital were suffering from the same thing, and some of them had died.

As her daughter lay there terribly sick, with others around her dying of the same illness, fear and worry came upon this mother like a storm, trying to overpower her mind and her emotions. The woman stepped out of the hospital room where her daughter lay, found a place where she could be alone, and prayed.

As she was praying, she said, "God, I can't do this. I am putting all my mental and emotional energy on You, and I am going to stand against fear." She began to speak to her fear — and the fear left her! With total confidence in the Lord, she then laid her hands on her child and prayed. Her daughter was healed and went home the next day.

Worry Is a Form of Pride

Friend, *you* have great power! *You* have an army of power inside you. First John 4:4 says, "You are of God, little children, and have overcome them, because He who is in you is greater than he who is in the world." Let go of your worries and put them into His hands. Let God have them!

Remember, worry is trusting in ourselves. It's a form of pride that says, "I can do this by myself, Lord." First Peter 5:5 says, "Likewise you younger people, submit yourselves to your elders. Yes, all of you be submissive to one another, and be clothed with humility, for 'God resists the proud, but gives grace to the humble.'" Notice that this verse tells us to "be clothed with humility." Why? Because God stands against the proud, but He draws close to the humble and gives them grace.

First Peter 5:6 goes on to say, "Therefore humble yourselves under the mighty hand of God, that He may exalt you in due time." There is much in this verse to learn from. If we know that God resists pride, then we must acknowledge our pride and say, "Lord, I'm sorry. I have been proud. I've been worrying and have not been trusting You with this situation. Lord, I give this to You."

We must be like the mother whose daughter was saved from that terrible disease. Instead of keeping her thoughts and emotions all to herself and worrying about the outcome, she humbled herself. And what did God do? He exalted her, and He raised up her daughter! That's the power we have when we humble ourselves. When we choose humility, we receive the grace and power of God that is there for us.

Humbly Cast Your Cares Upon the Lord

Continuing on in First Peter 5, verse 7 finally concludes by saying, "Casting all your care upon Him, for He cares for you." Casting our cares is a *decision* we make. Denise shared a story on the program about her grandson, William, as an example of deciding to cast our cares on God. She explained:

My grandson, William, was probably five years old at the time, and his sister was about three years old. Rick and I wanted to take him out to eat, to see a show, and to spend the whole day with him. All day long, my grandson was absolutely perfect in his behavior and actions. He didn't argue with his sister. He didn't say anything except, 'Yes,' and 'I'll do that,' and 'Thank you.' He was so perfect.

At the end of the day, I said to him, 'I just have to tell you, thank you so much. This has been a wonderful day with you today, and you were just so amazing and obedient. What did you do?'

My grandson replied, 'Well, Grandma, I have two buttons. I have one in the front and one in the back. My disobedient button is the one in the back. So I just turned that button off, and I turned on my obedient button.' It changed his whole attitude!

Friend, choosing to obey God is a *decision*. Yes, we need the Word of God. We need the knowledge and power that it gives us to increase our faith. And then *we* have to take that step to obey it. Denise's friend had to *agree* with the power of God so she could see her daughter raised up from sickness. Little William had to take the step to turn off the "disobedient button" and turn on the "obedient button." When we obey, we *choose* to do it.

We Are Empowered To Obey God's Word

Obeying God's Word and casting your cares onto Him is a *choice* — but you don't take this step by yourself. You are *empowered* by the Holy Spirit to make this choice and recognize that worrying is not productive. It's like a treadmill keeping you busy, going around and around, but never arriving at a destination. This is what happens if you embrace worry.

But you can embrace the power of God! It's there for you right now. Cast your cares onto the Lord, turn them over to Him, and acknowledge that He is able to handle them. He has not called you to carry a heavy burden. His yoke is easy and His burden is light (*see* Matthew 11:30).

Friend, this is one of the most powerful biblical truths that we can grab hold of. There are people who are sick in their *physical bodies* because they're worried, but Jesus has given us the answer. We can lean upon Him, just as Denise leaned on her son Paul when she climbed up the mountainside to view Noah's Ark. We can get through the situations we are in, not by leaning on ourselves, but by leaning on God.

Receive this word right now and tell God, "Lord, I can't carry this anymore. I humble myself right now, and I lay it at Your feet." This is a powerful act of faith, and you can do it because He told you to do it. He has given you the power — the mighty army within you by the Holy Spirit — to do what He said. Let this word penetrate deep within you, so you can conquer worry. It may be a process to cast your cares upon the Lord, but it's a process that you can win! You have the victory!

STUDY QUESTIONS

Be diligent to present yourself approved to God, a worker
who does not need to be ashamed, rightly dividing the word of truth.
— 2 Timothy 2:15

1. Worry knocks on everyone's door; it is a temptation every person faces. What does First Corinthians 10:13 tell us about temptation?

2. Worry drags us into a downward spiral of our own thoughts, which can get us in trouble and prevent us from walking in the peace that God purchased for us. How can we exchange worry for God's peace? (*Consider* Isaiah 26:3 and Philippians 4:6-7.)

3. God invites you to lean on Him rather than leaning on yourself. What will happen if you truly have faith in God? (*Consider* Mark 11:22-24; Romans 5:1; and Galatians 2:20.)

PRACTICAL APPLICATION

But be doers of the word,
and not hearers only, deceiving yourselves.
— James 1:22

1. When we worry, it's as if we're keeping our problem in our *own* hands. And if our need is in *our* hands, it is not in *His* hands. Take a few moments to look objectively at yourself. Are you holding onto your problems, or have you placed them into God's hands? If you're trying to conquer things on your own, repent and turn them over to the Lord instead.

2. In the program, Denise gave us the key to "crush worry." We are to bring our problems out of the arena of our mind, quit dwelling on them, and bring them into the arena of faith. First John 5:4 says, "For whatever is born of God overcomes the world. And this is the victory that has overcome the world — our faith." You overcome this world *by faith*! And you overcome worry *by faith*! Take time now to say *no* to worrying thoughts, shutting them off so you can focus your thoughts on the truth of God's Word.

3. Have you been worried about your physical body? *Jesus* is your Healer! He paid the price for your healing. According to Isaiah 53:5, "…He was wounded for our transgressions, He was bruised for our iniquities; the chastisement for our peace was upon Him, and by His stripes we

are healed." Receive your healing today. Pray this from your heart: *Dear Lord, Jesus, thank You for paying the price for my healing. I receive You as my Healer today, and I receive what You did for me now. Thank You for healing me! In Jesus' name. Amen.*

TOPIC

What Does Jesus Say About Worry?

SCRIPTURES

1. **Hebrews 2:18** — For in that He Himself has suffered, being tempted, He is able to aid those who are tempted.

2. **Hebrews 4:15-16** — For we do not have a High Priest who cannot sympathize with our weaknesses, but was in all points tempted as we are, yet without sin. Let us therefore come boldly to the throne of grace, that we may obtain mercy and find grace to help in time of need.

3. **Matthew 6:25-27** — Therefore I say to you, do not worry about your life, what you will eat or what you will drink; nor about your body, what you will put on. Is not life more than food and the body more than clothing? Look at the birds of the air, for they neither sow nor reap nor gather into barns; yet your heavenly Father feeds them. Are you not of more value than they? Which of you by worrying can add one cubit to his stature?

4. **Luke 12:6-7** — Are not five sparrows sold for two copper coins? And not one of them is forgotten before God. But the very hairs of your head are all numbered. Do not fear therefore; you are of more value than many sparrows.

5. **Hebrews 1:3** — Who being the brightness of His glory and the express image of His person, and upholding all things by the word of His power, when He had by Himself purged our sins, sat down at the right hand of the Majesty on high.

6. **Matthew 6:28-34** — So why do you worry about clothing? Consider the lilies of the field, how they grow: they neither toil nor spin; and yet I say to you that even Solomon in all his glory was not arrayed

like one of these. Now if God so clothes the grass of the field, which today is, and tomorrow is thrown into the oven, will He not much more clothe you, O you of little faith? Therefore do not worry, saying, "What shall we eat?" or "What shall we drink?" or "What shall we wear?" For after all these things the Gentiles seek. For your heavenly Father knows that you need all these things. But seek first the kingdom of God and His righteousness, and all these things shall be added to you. Therefore do not worry about tomorrow, for tomorrow will worry about its own things. Sufficient for the day is its own trouble.

SYNOPSIS

Jesus commands us not to worry, and He has given us the power to walk free from it. The same God who feeds the birds and clothes the flowers in such detailed beauty cares even more for us! He treasures us as His prized children. He knows our needs intimately and promises to meet them with His loving care. When we seek Him first, we are empowered to cast off worry, embrace His peace, and trust that He will handle every detail of our lives.

The emphasis of this lesson:

We are called to live free from worry, being confident that our Heavenly Father knows our needs and will provide for us. Worry is fruitless and steals our peace, but when we seek God first and trust in Him, we can walk in His supernatural care. By turning away from anxious thoughts and agreeing with God's promises, we can embrace the peace and victory He has already given us.

Worry touches all our lives. We may feel like we are stuck dealing with it, but the good news is that Jesus instructed us not to worry. And Jesus would never tell us to do something if He didn't also give us the power to do what He said. Yes, we live in a world that's dominated by anxiety. We are taught to worry and told that there is something wrong with us if we don't. So we need godly equipment to stand against it. We must know *what Jesus says about worry* — so that we can successfully resist worry and walk in peace instead.

Watch Out for the Temptation To Worry

Did you know that Jesus was tempted to worry just as we are? That's why He is compassionate toward us when we face this temptation. According to Hebrews 2:18, He knows what it's like to be tempted and He's *able* to help those who are tempted. You see, He loves us so much that He came and lived on Earth, knowing that He would be tempted just like we are.

Many times Jesus was called a blasphemer (*see* Luke 5:21; John 10:33). Jesus was also accused of getting His power from the prince of demons, the devil, and being a drunkard. Matthew 12:24 says, "Now when the Pharisees heard it they said, 'This fellow does not cast out demons except by Beelzebub, the ruler of the demons.'" And Luke 7:34 says, "The Son of Man has come eating and drinking, and you say, 'Look, a glutton and a winebibber, a friend of tax collectors and sinners!'"

Jesus endured so much in this world, and He certainly understands what it's like to be tempted with worry. Before you consider what Jesus said about worry, remember that He is able to aid you if you come to Him. He is not the God with a clenched fist — He is the God with an open hand, and He offers you His help.

Hebrews 4:15 and 16 says, "For we do not have a High Priest who cannot sympathize with our weaknesses, but was in all points tempted as we are, yet without sin. Let us therefore come boldly to the throne of grace, that we may obtain mercy and find grace to help in time of need." Jesus was tempted just as we are — yet *without sin.*

The first part of this verse says that "we do not have a High Priest who cannot sympathize." Jesus *can* and *does* sympathize with us. He was tempted in the very same way that we are tempted to worry. Yet, as we will see throughout this lesson, in the Word of God, Jesus instructs us not to worry. And rest assured, if He commands us to do it, He *has* equipped us to overcome and resist the temptation to worry.

'Do Not Worry About Your Life'

In Matthew 6:25-27, Jesus declares, "Therefore I say to you, do not worry about your life, what you will eat or what you will drink; nor about your body, what you will put on. Is not life more than food and the body more than clothing? Look at the birds of the air, for they neither sow nor reap nor gather into barns; yet your heavenly Father feeds them. Are you not of more value than they? Which of you by worrying can add one cubit to his stature?"

In these verses, Jesus tells us that we are not to fret about what we will eat, drink, or wear. He reminds us that worry is fruitless. Let's look again at verse 26: "Look at the birds of the air, for they neither sow nor reap nor gather into barns; yet your heavenly Father feeds them. Are you not of more value than they?" Birds don't sit around and worry. They don't gather, and they don't reap. Yet the Lord takes care of them.

Are you not much more valuable than the birds? Of course you are! Luke 12:6 and 7 says, "Are not five sparrows sold for two copper coins? And not one of them is forgotten before God. But the very hairs of your head are all numbered. Do not fear therefore; you are of more value than many sparrows."

God the Father is holding all the earth together, all matter, and all the atoms and protons — in fact, He is "upholding all things by the word of His power" (Hebrews 1:3). The same God who holds the universe together sees when a bird falls out of a tree (*see* Matthew 10:29-31). Imagine how much more our mighty God cares about *you*!

Matthew 6:27 says, "Which of you by worrying can add one cubit to his stature?" Jesus compares the act of fretting about what will happen in different situations of our lives to trying to plan hard enough to add inches to our height. How could we ever sit and strategize long enough to get taller? It's impossible. According to Jesus, worrying about our life in this way is just as unfruitful.

Instead of worrying, Jesus encourages us to look at the birds. Notice how calmly they sit on wires or on a tree branch. Have you ever seen a bird have a nervous breakdown? No — because they know that their heavenly Father is taking care of them. It is powerful to know that your heavenly Father is taking care of you.

Seek Him and He Will Add to You

In Matthew 6:28-30, Jesus says, "So why do you worry about clothing? Consider the lilies of the field, how they grow: they neither toil nor spin; and yet I say to you that even Solomon in all his glory was not arrayed like one of these. Now if God so clothes the grass of the field, which today is, and tomorrow is thrown into the oven, will He not much more clothe you, O you of little faith?"

The flowers we see are made and adorned by God. The lilies grow and are tended by Him, and their beauty is greater than Solomon in all his glory. How much more is your magnificent God, who clothes these insignificant flowers, going to clothe you?

Matthew 6:31-33 goes on to declare, "Therefore do not worry, saying, 'What shall we eat?' or 'What shall we drink?' or 'What shall we wear?' For after all these things the Gentiles seek. For your heavenly Father knows that you need all these things. But seek first the kingdom of God and His righteousness, and all these things shall be added to you."

God knows our needs. And He tells us that if we seek Him, He will add "all these things" to our lives. But first, we must get our eyes off those things, off our worries, and turn our eyes to the Lord. In doing so, we can see and declare, "You're my heavenly Father. You love me. You're going to take care of me." As our faith in Him arises, we don't worry. We see, as Jesus said, that these things will be added to us. They'll be added to us without the stress of trying to do it ourselves.

Let God Carry Your Cares About Tomorrow

Finally, Matthew 6:34 concludes, "Therefore do not worry about tomorrow, for tomorrow will worry about its own things. Sufficient for the day is its own trouble." Jesus tells us not to worry about tomorrow. Friend, Jesus knew what His tomorrow held. Because of prophecy, He knew that He would be tortured, that they would pull His beard out, and that He would be struggling for breath on the Cross. He knew it all.

Jesus knew He was going to be separated from His Father and go to hell for us, and He knew He would be raised from the dead. But remember, He was tempted in the same way we are. Yes, Jesus could have worried about it, but He didn't.

So often, we worry about our lives, our relationships, or whether we will have enough money. We may worry about our clothes, or what we will eat and drink. In the midst of this, God says, "Don't you know that I care for you? I care for you more than the flowers and the birds. Don't worry about tomorrow."

Denise shared that she has meditated on this verse for hours because in her own life, she has been tempted to worry. Matthew 6:34 says, "Don't worry about tomorrow." When we worry about tomorrow, we waste our mental energy. But if we don't worry about tomorrow, we can live fully each day. As we live fully in the present, we will do everything we are supposed to do for tomorrow. We will have the power, the mental ability, and the emotional ability to complete *tomorrow* because we have used our *today* properly.

Worry Is a Terrible Enemy

Have you ever worried and worried and then realized you were exhausted from worry? Denise shared that she knew two people who became sick through worrying. One of the women had cancer, and she told Denise, "I know I opened the door to this cancer because I worried so much about if God was going to provide [financially] for me." The other woman was so worried about her son that she had a heart attack.

Worry is not our friend. Worry is an *enemy*, and we need to treat it that way. When anxious thoughts come across our mind or try to work in our emotions, we must put up a door and say, "No, worry! You're not coming in." The Word of God says that He cares for us more than birds, more than flowers, and we are His. He loves us, and we can seek Him, and He will do the work. We don't have to stress over it. He will add to us what we need.

We are to *agree* with God. It is not enough to know what Matthew 6:31-34 says. We must *do* what this passage of Scripture says — and *agree* with God. We are to declare by faith, "God, I agree with You. I am not going to worry about tomorrow. I am going to live today to its fullest, and I will be ready for tomorrow and the next day."

Worry steals our time, and we will not get that time back. So we ought to take the opportunity that God has given us right now to live today to the fullest. Worry is a thief — it's a lie. It's an enemy. But we can see in the Word of God that Jesus was tempted in all points as we are, yet without sin. And He has given us the Holy Spirit so we can overcome the enemy of worry.

Agree With God and Turn Away From Worry

Friend, you can have peace *today*. You can say no to worrying thoughts and emotions because your God is taking care of you. That's a powerful statement! Declare it right now: *My God loves me, and He's going to take care of me. I belong to Him, and He lives in me.*

It is powerful to switch on your agreement with God and turn off everything that disagrees with Him. Remember, worry steals your peace. But God paid an amazing price through Jesus to give you the peace that's inside you right now by the Holy Spirit. His peace that passes understanding is one of the fruits of the Spirit inside you. And you can exchange your worry for His peace. You can say goodbye to worry! You can say hello to peace and agree with the power of God that's inside you!

STUDY QUESTIONS

**Be diligent to present yourself approved to God, a worker
who does not need to be ashamed, rightly dividing the word of truth.
— 2 Timothy 2:15**

1. Jesus knew He would be separated from His Father and go to the Cross for us. He also knew He would be raised from the dead. But since He was tempted in every way we are (*see* Hebrews 4:15), is it possible He was tempted to worry? Why or why not?

2. Read Luke 12:22-32. Verse 32 reads, "Do not fear, little flock, for it is your Father's good pleasure to give you the kingdom." How does knowing that it's your Father's *good* pleasure to give you the Kingdom change the way you view your worries and fears?

3. This lesson made several things clear about worry. Which of these impacted you most?

   • Worry is not a friend. Worry is an *enemy*, and we need to treat it that way.

   • When anxious thoughts come across your mind or try to work in your emotions, resist them by saying, "No, worry! You're not coming in."

   • Worry is a thief. It wastes mental energy.

   • The Bible says that God cares for you more than birds and flowers, and you are *His*.

   • God loves you! You can seek Him, and He will do the work.

   • You don't have to stress over problems. The Lord will give you what you need.

PRACTICAL APPLICATION

But be doers of the word,
and not hearers only, deceiving yourselves.
— James 1:22

1. Maybe you are struggling with sickness and disease right now. Remember, Jesus is your Healer. Every drop of blood that came from His body has your salvation, deliverance, and healing in it. Your healing is in His Blood, and His Blood is powerful *today*. You can turn away from worry and say yes to peace and healing. Thank Him right now for the power of His Blood.

2. Matthew 6:34 says, "…Do not worry about tomorrow.…" In the program, Denise taught that when you worry about tomorrow, you waste mental energy. But if you don't worry about tomorrow, you can live today fully. As you live totally in the present, you will have the power, the mental ability, and the emotional strength to complete tomorrow successfully because you have used your today properly. How did you use today? Did you find yourself worrying? Take time to meditate on Matthew 6:34. Write it out and place it where you can see it regularly as a reminder not to worry.

3. According to James 1:22-25, walking in victory over worry is not just about hearing God's Word, it's about *doing* it! Make the heart adjustment to agree with God's Word and *do it*. Say this from your heart: *God, I agree with You. I choose to do Your Word. I am not going to worry about tomorrow, and I am going to live today to its fullest by Your grace. I will be ready for tomorrow. In Jesus' name. Amen.*

TOPIC

Make a New Habit, Leave Worry Behind

SCRIPTURES

1. **Matthew 11:28-30** — Come to Me, all you who labor and are heavy laden, and I will give you rest. Take My yoke upon you and learn from Me, for I am gentle and lowly in heart, and you will find rest for your souls. For My yoke is easy and My burden is light.

2. **2 Corinthians 10:4-5** — For the weapons of our warfare are not carnal but mighty in God for pulling down strongholds, casting down arguments and every high thing that exalts itself against the knowledge of God, bringing every thought into captivity to the obedience of Christ.

3. **Ephesians 2:6** — And raised us up together, and made us sit together in the heavenly places in Christ Jesus.

4. **2 Timothy 1:7** — For God has not given us a spirit of fear, but of power and of love and of a sound mind.

5. **Isaiah 53:5** — But He was wounded for our transgressions, He was bruised for our iniquities; the chastisement for our peace was upon Him, and by His stripes we are healed.

6. **Matthew 19:6** — So then, they are no longer two but one flesh. Therefore what God has joined together, let not man separate.

7. **Matthew 4:1** — Then Jesus was led up by the Spirit into the wilderness to be tempted by the devil.

8. **James 4:7** — Therefore submit to God. Resist the devil and he will flee from you.

9. **1 Peter 5:7-8** — Casting all your care upon Him, for He cares for you. Be sober, be vigilant; because your adversary the devil walks about like a roaring lion, seeking whom he may devour.

10. **Proverbs 23:29-35** — Who has woe? Who has sorrow? Who has contentions? Who has complaints? Who has wounds without cause? Who has redness of eyes? Those who linger long at the wine, those

who go in search of mixed wine. Do not look on the wine when it is red, when it sparkles in the cup, when it swirls around smoothly; at the last it bites like a serpent, and stings like a viper. Your eyes will see strange things, and your heart will utter perverse things. Yes, you will be like one who lies down in the midst of the sea, or like one who lies at the top of the mast, saying: "They have struck me, but I was not hurt; they have beaten me, but I did not feel it. When shall I awake, that I may seek another drink?"

11. **James 4:8** — Draw near to God and He will draw near to you. Cleanse your hands, you sinners; and purify your hearts, you double-minded.

SYNOPSIS

You don't have to be a slave to worry! Just as worry can become a habit, so can resisting it and walking in God's peace instead. Through the power of His Word, you can pull down strongholds, cast off anxious thoughts, and take hold of the victory that belongs to you in Christ. When you cast your cares on the Lord, He fills you with His wisdom, power, and perfect peace — empowering you to rise up, take authority, and leave worry behind for good.

The emphasis of this lesson:

Worry can become a habit, but through God's Word, you have the power to break free and walk in His peace. By casting down anxious thoughts, resisting the enemy, and trusting in God's constant care, you can replace worry with faith. When you release your burdens to Him, He fills your life with His wisdom, strength, and supernatural peace.

Do you know that you can resist worry? Many people believe they are a slave to worry without any control over it. But living this way can steal our health. We weren't made to carry worry. Jesus said in Matthew 11:28-30, "Come to Me, all you who labor and are heavy laden, and I will give you rest. Take My yoke upon you and learn from Me, for I am gentle and lowly in heart, and you will find rest for your souls. For My yoke is easy and My burden is light." He desires to take our heavy burdens so we can live in peace rather than in worry.

Resist the Habit of Worrying

We can be free from worry, but first we must recognize that worry can become habitual. When a subject arises that worries us, it is as if we turn on a switch and find ourselves in the same old thought patterns. It gets us every time and turns on our anxious thoughts. Worrying can be a habit, just like brushing our teeth. We hold our toothbrush in a certain way and use a certain toothpaste because we have become accustomed to it. Similarly, when a particular subject touches our life, a whole string of thoughts can arise. It's a *habit* to worry about that topic.

When worrying is a habit, it can become a stronghold. Anxious thoughts can open a door for the enemy to come in and steal our peace over and over again. Friend, he doesn't have any right to our peace! Jesus paid the price for us to have peace, and He put His Holy Spirit inside us. One fruit of the Spirit is peace (*see* Galatians 5:22-23). So we have *a right to peace*.

If you have a stronghold of worry, you can pull it down. Second Corinthians 10:4 and 5 says, "For the weapons of our warfare are not carnal but mighty in God for pulling down strongholds, casting down arguments and every high thing that exalts itself against the knowledge of God, bringing every thought into captivity to the obedience of Christ." If you worry and fret, you may even believe that you are right to do so. And sometimes a door to sickness can open in your life because you're worried. Worry is a stronghold that you ought to pull down!

The Bible says, "...the weapons of our warfare are not carnal but mighty..." (2 Corinthians 10:4). They're mighty through God! Look at what these weapons can do! They are "...mighty in God for pulling down strongholds, casting down arguments and every high thing that exalts itself against the knowledge of God, bringing every thought into captivity to the obedience of Christ" (2 Corinthians 10:4-5). The language in these verses shows that you're not the victim. *You're the victor!* You're the one with the power to pull down strongholds and bring worrisome thoughts into captivity.

How To Bring Down the Stronghold of Worry

Notice the beginning of Second Corinthians 10:5, which says, "...casting down arguments and every high thing that exalts itself against the knowledge of God...." How do we cast down the habit of worry? We can do it by acting on what the Bible instructs us to do. When an anxious thought comes, we can tell ourselves, "I'm not going to receive that." Then, we cast the thought *down*. Why *down*? The Bible says that the enemy is *under our feet*.

Ephesians 2:6 says, "And [God] raised us up together, and made us sit together in the heavenly places in Christ Jesus." We are seated in heavenly places with Christ Jesus, and the enemy is under our feet. When we cast down a thought, we put it right where it belongs — under our feet. We are not under its authority, but the thought is under *our* authority. We have power! We don't have to be subject to worry, feeling we can't do anything about it. That is absolutely not true. We can cast down *every* thought that exalts itself against the knowledge of God.

You may ask, "Do I have to cast down *every* thought?" The question is, do you really want some thoughts of worry to stay in your mind? No! So cast down every thought that does not align with God's Word. When such a thought comes, you can say, "No, I'm not taking that." Declare God's Word instead.

When fear comes, we can declare Second Timothy 1:7, which says, "For God has not given us a spirit of fear, but of power and of love and of a sound mind." When worries about sickness come, Isaiah 53:5 says, "But He was wounded for our transgressions, He was bruised for our iniquities; the chastisement for our peace was upon Him, and by His stripes we are healed."

When concern over our children arises, we can say, "The Bible says that my child, my seed, is the blessed of the Lord (*see* Psalm 37:25-26). Devil, you take your hands off my child." When stress comes into our marriage, we can say, "Devil, you're not destroying my marriage. I cast down that thought because the Bible says, '…Therefore what God has joined together, let not man separate'" (Matthew 19:6). This is practical instruction!

The Word of God Is Mighty Against Worry

After Jesus had fasted for 40 days in the wilderness, the enemy came to tempt him. We read about this in Matthew 4:1, which declares, "Then Jesus was led up by the Spirit into the wilderness to be tempted by the devil." When that happened, Jesus didn't argue with the devil — He simply quoted the Word of God. Friend, if it's good enough for Jesus to quote the Word of God against the devil and put him on the run, it is good enough for us!

In fact, James 4:7 tells us, "Therefore submit to God. Resist the devil and he will flee from you." We have resisting power. We have power to cast down thoughts of worry. If our worries have been habitual, then we must

be habitual in casting those thoughts down and speaking the Word of God over our lives.

Consider the remaining part of Second Corinthians 10:5, which says, "...bringing every thought into captivity to the obedience of Christ." Again, we see that we are the ones with the power. We are the ones bringing every thought into captivity to the obedience of Christ. In the Greek language, this verse offers the picture of *a man who has a sword plunged into his enemy's back*. The man is saying, "I'm not moving. *You* are moving."

When a particular scripture rises up inside you or you speak a specific scripture over your situation, this is what is known as a *rhema* — a specific, spoken Word of God for a specific situation. This is the exact Greek word used in Ephesians 6:17, where it describes the sword of the Spirit. We can use the Word of God like a sword, and through this *rhema*, spoken Word of God, we can say, "No, devil, you're not doing that." Poke the sword right into his back and tell him, "I'm taking these thoughts captive, and you will not talk to me that way."

You may ask, "Do people really do this?" Yes! We *have* to do it. We don't want to live under the habitual thoughts of worry. We want to enjoy the peace that God has given us. The peace that passes all understanding is on the inside of our wonderful, born-again spirit. It's all the peace we're ever going to need! But we have a part to play in our victory. We are to pull down worrying thoughts, not letting them run us around. We are to put the sword of God's Word in the back of our enemy and say, "You will listen to me. I'm the one with the authority here."

Be Sober About the Enemy of Worry

In First Peter 5:7 and 8, we read, "Casting all your care upon Him, for He cares for you. Be sober, be vigilant; because your adversary the devil walks about like a roaring lion, seeking whom he may devour." The enemy, our adversary, wants to devour us. But when we're casting our cares on the Lord, he can't do it.

Rather than being drunk on worry, we are to stay sober, so we can see more clearly. When people are drunk, their vision is hindered. They don't see clearly because of the effects of the alcohol. We are to be sober and not allow the horrible habit of worry to take us down. Proverbs 23:29-35 says:

Who has woe? Who has sorrow? Who has contentions? Who has complaints? Who has wounds without cause? Who has redness of eyes? Those who linger long at the wine, those who go in search of mixed wine.

Do not look on the wine when it is red, when it sparkles in the cup, when it swirls around smoothly; at the last it bites like a serpent, and stings like a viper. Your eyes will see strange things, and your heart will utter perverse things.

Yes, you will be like one who lies down in the midst of the sea, or like one who lies at the top of the mast, saying: 'They have struck me, but I was not hurt; they have beaten me, but I did not feel it. When shall I awake, that I may seek another drink?'

The temptation to worry is just like what Proverbs 23:29-35 says about alcohol. Don't look at the sparkling red in the cup — look at what happens in the end. This passage of Scripture ends with, "When shall I awake, that I may seek another drink?" Our spirit is filled with peace, but our flesh is an enemy against our spirit — and our flesh wants to worry. Our flesh is so habitual that it's as if it wakes up and says, "When is my next opportunity to worry about this?"

Jesus paid the complete price for us to enjoy His peace. And He instructs us to be sober. Don't be intoxicated on worry. Don't let anxiety tell you how you will act, think, or feel. You have been given the power to say no to it. You have been given the power, as it says in Second Corinthians 10:4 and 5, to cast down those thoughts of worry.

Take Your Stand and Agree With God

You may have worried a long time about a particular thing in your life. If so, it's good to be honest about it, because if you are honest with God, then He and you can do something about it. You can agree with God, now that you see that worrying is not His will for you. Just because people in your life have been worriers doesn't mean you must be that way also. You have the Holy Spirit in you, and you can overcome. You can cast down those thoughts. Take the Word of God like a sword, stick it in the back of anxious thoughts, and say, "No! You're coming down now. You're not going to rule me anymore."

When we do this, when we agree with God, then we can start to have the thoughts of God. Remember that when we're worried, it's like we have the situation in *our* hands, saying, "*I'm* going to figure this out. *I've* got this in my hands. *I'm* going to fret about it some more." But if it's in *our* hands, then it's not in *His* hands.

We need God's power, His grace, and His wisdom to address our problem, rather than just our own ability. He doesn't want us carrying the heavy burden of worry. Look again at First Peter 5:7: "Casting all your care upon Him, for He cares for you." One commentary says this verse means He is constantly caring for you — *constantly*! Every concern that drops by our brain or our emotions, God constantly cares about it. He is waiting for us to cast our worries on Him, so that we can receive His care.

You may say, "I don't think it's that simple. I've been worrying for a long time." Today is a good day to say, "God, I don't want this habit anymore. Lord, I repent. Holy Spirit, help me." And because He's the Helper, He can bring you help. He can give you wisdom, grace, and knowledge — and He can cause you to have a *new* thought. He brings answers when we seek Him.

James 4:8 admonishes, "Draw near to God and He will draw near to you...." When we draw near to Him, we receive what He has. When we cast our care on Him, our hands are emptied — and we are able to receive from Him. We do not have to be ruled by worry and care. We can receive His peace, His answers, and the power that Jesus paid an amazing price to give us. We can cast our care upon the Lord because He cares for us.

Take the load of care and worry that has been in your hands, and by your own will and in accordance with His Word, cast it on the Lord. It's not yours. Receive His answers. Receive His power, in the name of Jesus. Remember, you are not the victim — you are the victor! You are more than a conqueror through Him who loves you, and you can overcome worry.

STUDY QUESTIONS

Be diligent to present yourself approved to God, a worker
who does not need to be ashamed, rightly dividing the word of truth.
— 2 Timothy 2:15

1. Many people believe they are a slave to worry and allow it to control them. But you don't have to be a slave to worry! Just as worry can become a habit, so can resisting it and walking in God's peace. What is your part in putting worry on the run and letting God's peace rule in your heart instead? (*Consider* Colossians 3:15; James 4:7; and First Peter 5:7-9.)

2. You can cast off anxious thoughts and take hold of the victory that belongs to you in Christ. Who is in charge of your thoughts? What should you do if a worrisome thought presents itself? (*Consider* 2 Corinthians 10:3-5.)

3. When you cast down worry or anxious thoughts, you are bringing those thoughts right where they belong — under your feet. You are not under the authority of worry. It is under *your* authority. (*Consider* Ephesians 1:22-23; and Ephesians 2:4-6.)

PRACTICAL APPLICATION

**But be doers of the word,
and not hearers only, deceiving yourselves.
— James 1:22**

1. Your physical body wasn't made to carry worry. If you've been a chronic worrier, the resulting stress could open the door to sickness or disease. Don't risk the trouble worry can cause! Repent of worrying and ask God to forgive you for carrying your own cares.

2. When you cast your cares on Him, your hands are emptied — you're no longer trying to solve your own problems. And once you cast your cares on Him, He moves to bring about the answers you need. Take time now to praise God that He is moving in your situation. By faith, thank the Lord because you have the victory in this situation, in Jesus' name!

3. James 4:8 says, "Draw near to God and He will draw near to you." When you draw near to Him, you position yourself to receive what He has. One way to draw near to the Lord is to worship Him. Lift your voice in worship to the One who said:
   • "If you abide in Me, and My words abide in you, you will ask what you desire, and it shall be done for you" (John 15:7).
   • "...I, the Lord your God, will hold your right hand, saying to you, 'Fear not, I will help you'" (Isaiah 41:13).

• "…I have loved you with an everlasting love…" (Jeremiah 31:3).

TOPIC
'What Is the Harm If I Just Worry a Little?'

SCRIPTURES

1. **Isaiah 41:10** — Fear not, for I am with you; be not dismayed, for I am your God. I will strengthen you, yes, I will help you, I will uphold you with My righteous right hand.

2. **Matthew 6:27** — Which of you by worrying can add one cubit to his stature?

3. **1 John 4:4** — You are of God, little children, and have overcome them, because He who is in you is greater than he who is in the world.

4. **1 Peter 5:8** — Be sober, be vigilant; because your adversary the devil walks about like a roaring lion, seeking whom he may devour.

5. **Proverbs 23:35** — They have struck me, but I was not hurt; they have beaten me, but I did not feel it. When shall I awake, that I may seek another drink?

6. **John 10:10** — The thief does not come except to steal, and to kill, and to destroy. I have come that they may have life, and that they may have it more abundantly.

7. **James 4:7** — Therefore submit to God. Resist the devil and he will flee from you.

8. **Matthew 11:28-30** — Come to Me, all you who labor and are heavy laden, and I will give you rest. Take My yoke upon you and learn from Me, for I am gentle and lowly in heart, and you will find rest for your souls. For My yoke is easy and My burden is light.

9. **1 Peter 5:7** — Casting all your care upon Him, for He cares for you.

10. **Revelation 1:17** — And when I saw Him, I fell at His feet as dead. But He laid His right hand on me, saying to me, "Do not be afraid; I am the First and the Last."

SYNOPSIS

Even a little worry can be detrimental to our lives. The Bible reminds us that we must not tolerate worry, because when we do, it opens the door for the devil to steal, kill, and destroy. While worrying is unfruitful, turning to God's Word and casting our cares on Jesus is a powerful way to address the things that concern us. By resisting the devil and giving our cares to God, we are empowered to receive His peace and His answers.

The emphasis of this lesson:

The habit of worrying can cause you to fall into the devil's trap — allowing him to deceive you and lead you into trouble. God's answer to worry is giving your cares to Him. When you refuse to let the devil lead you and, instead, give your concerns to the Lord in faith, you are freed from the heavy burden of worry and find true rest and peace for your soul.

You have the power to tell worry goodbye! In fact, you can renew your mind to the Word of God so much that you understand you are not a slave or a victim to worry, but instead, you are a victor over it. This is good news! You do not have to entertain even a little worry. It is important that you keep grabbing hold of the victory so you can have a mind that is peaceful. The world is searching for peace, but as a born-again believer, peace has been purchased for you by the blood of Jesus. His peace is in your born-again spirit right now, and you can have victory over every little bit of worry that tries to come against you.

We Must Let Go of Worry

In Lesson 1 of this series, we learned that *worry is keeping things out of God's hands and keeping them in our hands.* It is deciding that we will not give God an issue, but we will keep hold of it and worry about it ourselves. But Isaiah 41:10 says, "Fear not, for I am with you; be not dismayed, for I am your God. I will strengthen you, yes, I will help you, I will uphold you with My righteous right hand." God wants to hold us, support us, and help us. If we have worry we're holding onto, He offers us His righteous right hand, ready to carry our cares for us.

In Lesson 2, we learned *what Jesus says about worry.* In Matthew 6:27, Jesus says, "Which of you by worrying can add one cubit to his stature?" He compares how fruitless worry is to the act of wishing that we could be taller. We could sit for hours thinking about it, write out a strategy about it, or talk to our friends about it — but these things will never cause us to grow taller. That's how fruitless worry is.

Then in Lesson 3, we learned that *worry can be habitual*. A worry can say, "I've been here a long time. I have a right to be here. I have my own residence here in your heart and mind. Don't touch that part of your soul. I've got that." But First John 4:4 says, "You are of God, little children, and have overcome them, because He who is in you is greater than he who is in the world." *If worry is a habit, it's a stronghold*. But we can pull down this stronghold with the mighty power of God that's inside us.

Next, in this lesson, we'll look at the danger of even a little worry. Sometimes we give *most* of our cares and concerns to God, and then keep a little bit to ourselves. But even a little worry can cause great harm. And the truth is, *Jesus doesn't want us to have even a little bit of worry*. He wants us to be completely free. He wants us to have the peace of God which passes all understanding and guards our hearts and minds (*see* Philippians 4:7).

Holding On To Worry Can Be Dangerous

To illustrate the problem with keeping even a little worry instead of placing it *all* in the Lord's hands, Denise shared two examples of people she knows who held onto worry. The results for both people were serious health problems.

One woman admitted that she worried so much about her financial situation that she developed cancer in her body. Today she is finished with the treatments and is completely cancer-free, but she told Denise, "I know that I opened the door to that cancer with my worry." Another woman told Denise that she worried so much about her child that it caused her to have a heart attack. This is not God's will! We can't hold onto even a little bit of worry — because a little bit will try to take over.

Proverbs 23:35 says, "They have struck me, but I was not hurt; they have beaten me, but I did not feel it. When shall I awake, that I may seek another drink?" Drunkenness is so much like habitual worrying. We can become drunk on worry, and it can take us over. God's will is that we're not overtaken by worry — *but that we resist it!*

Be Alert Against the Enemy's Lies

The adversary is like a roaring lion, walking around seeking who he might devour. He can't devour everybody — but he's seeking those who are overcome with worry, those who are drunk on it. First Peter 5:8 says, "Be sober, be vigilant; because your adversary the devil walks about like a roaring lion, seeking whom he may devour." To be vigilant means *to be alert*. We are to stay awake and alert, because the adversary is searching for those individuals who are drunk on worry and aren't sober, vigilant, or alert.

The devil's name means *slanderer*. He slanders us and tells us lies about ourselves and other people. His lies never lift us up — they put us down. The Bible compares him to a lion — one of the most ferocious animals. Take a moment to picture the continual roaring of Satan as a lion walking about, seeking his prey. When First Peter 5:8 says that he is "seeking whom he may devour," the word "devour" is a violent word that means the devil wants *to swallow up, to eat it up*, and *to devour* us. It literally means *to drink down*, like an animal swallowing its prey. This is exactly what the enemy wants to do to us.

John 10:10 says, "The thief does not come except to steal, and to kill, and to destroy. I have come that they may have life, and that they may have it more abundantly." Jesus came to give us life — and life "more abundantly." But the devil — the thief — comes only to steal, kill, and destroy. When we worry, even just a little bit, we are opening the door to the devourer, to the slanderer.

Shut the Door on the Devil's Deceit

As a result of worrying, people can start to believe the devil's lies. They begin to believe the worries and complaints. It gets into their bodies and their emotions, and they become deceived by the lies. As a result, they begin to act in the wrong ways. We may think to ourselves, *How could this person who has walked so closely with God be acting like this now? I don't understand.* It's a process that happens slowly when we open the door to the slanderer.

What does it look like when we open a door to the enemy? Here's an example: Imagine that the enemy is slandering us and making accusations day and night repeatedly in our mind. We believe it, and we start to worry about it. We believe we have a right to those worries and cares, and we begin to have strong emotions about the situation. As we listen to these worrisome thoughts, the act becomes habitual. Worry begins to speak to us so much that we believe it and act on it — and then we become the deceived one.

Friend, the devil *wants to deceive us*. First Peter 5:8 says He is "seeking whom he may devour." He's looking for the one who is believing *wrong*, who is listening to his lies and has opened the door to him. That's how dangerous that worry is! It opens the door to the devil.

What should we do about this? We are to shut the door to the devil — which we can do because the Bible says we have authority over him. James 4:7 says, "Therefore submit to God. Resist the devil and he will flee from you." Resisting the devil is a *disciplinary action*. If you discipline your child, *you* are the one in authority, not the child. Friend, *you* take the disciplinary action — not the devil, not his lies. Don't allow him to run you around. Resist him, and he will flee from you.

James 4:7 confirms who it is that has the power. It's not the devil — it's you. *You are the one with the power.* You are the one with the say-so, the one with the authority who can declare, "Devil, you get out of my thoughts. You get out of my emotions. I take authority over you. You have no right to me." You can shut the door on the devil and his accusations.

Jesus Wants Our Load To Be Light

Jesus is so tenderhearted toward us, and He cares about everything that we are carrying. Consider what He invites us to do when we're battling worry. Matthew 11:28-30 says, "Come to Me, all you who labor and are heavy laden, and I will give you rest. Take My yoke upon you and learn from Me, for I am gentle and lowly in heart, and you will find rest for your souls. For My yoke is easy and My burden is light." This is Jesus' invitation to each and every one of us.

He says, "Come to Me, all you who labor and are heavy laden…." He cares so much for us. In fact, First Peter 5:7 says, "Casting all your care upon Him, *for He cares for you.*" What will He do when we come to Him and hand over all our burdens, cares, and worries? He will give us rest. This is the great exchange! We may be heavy laden and carrying many burdens, but Jesus declares, "Come to Me! Come to Me, and I will give you rest." We give Him our heavy burdens, and *He gives us His rest.* It is so simple!

Jesus goes on to say in Matthew 11:28-30, "Take My yoke upon you and learn from Me, for I am gentle and lowly in heart, and you will find rest for your souls." Notice that He doesn't have a checklist, assessing what we have and have not done. No, He is gentle. He is lowly in heart and approachable.

Perhaps you know someone who is approachable, and you like them. He or she doesn't want anything from you, but you have an audience with him or her. Well, if Jesus appeared in your living room right now, you wouldn't find Him austere or prideful. He is powerful, but you would also find Him to be gentle and lowly in heart. When you meditate on who He really is and you come to Him, you can immediately find rest.

You Can Be Free From the Burden of Worry

Revelation 1:17 is a great example of how gentle and approachable Jesus is. In that verse, the apostle John was on the island of Patmos when he had a vision of Jesus. The Bible says, "And when I saw Him, I fell at His feet as dead. But He laid His right hand on me, saying to me, 'Do not be afraid; I am the First and the Last.'" Jesus touched John and said, "Do not be afraid." This is how He is right now toward us. Whatever situation we are dealing with, He wants to touch our lives with His tender love and say, "Don't worry about that. I've got it. Come to Me, and I'll give you the rest you're seeking."

Continuing on with Matthew 11, Jesus says in verse 30, "For My yoke is easy and My burden is light." Do you have a heavy burden? Do you know someone who does? According to Jesus, we shouldn't have to carry heavy burdens because His yoke is easy, and His burden is light. If we are carrying a heavy burden, then we're carrying it by ourselves. But if we're giving it to Him, the burden becomes light.

We have authority over worry! God wants us to be completely delivered and have His peace dominating and ruling in our hearts. Jesus doesn't want us to have even a *little* bit of worry that can open a door to the devil. He wants us to have complete freedom. His desire is that our hearts will be dominated, controlled, and empowered by peace. He wants to give us rest for our souls. This is the will of God for us.

STUDY QUESTIONS

Be diligent to present yourself approved to God, a worker
who does not need to be ashamed, rightly dividing the word of truth.
— 2 Timothy 2:15

1. Even a little bit of worry is not good to hold on to. Why? Because it will take over and become bigger. If we allow even a little worry to occupy our thoughts, we open the door to the devil, and he is a devourer and slanderer. Don't give him an inch by worrying even a tiny bit! (*Consider* Ephesians 4:27 and Ephesians 6:10-13.)

2. Revelation 12:10 calls the enemy "the accuser of our brethren, who accused them before our God day and night." Read the next verse! According to Revelation 12:11, how do we overcome?

3. Have you ever felt bombarded with wrong thoughts? Was the enemy behind this temptation? What does Luke 10:19 tell us about the authority God has given us over all the power of the enemy?

PRACTICAL APPLICATION

But be doers of the word,
and not hearers only, deceiving yourselves.
— James 1:22

1. This lesson opens our eyes to the opportunity for a great exchange. Jesus says, "Come to Me, all you who labor and are heavy laden, and I will give you rest" (Matthew 11:28). When we give Him our labor and heavy burdens, Jesus gives us *rest*. This is the great exchange! Pray this from your heart: *Lord Jesus, I come to You now for the great exchange. I give You the burdens I've been carrying and receive Your rest. Thank You, precious Lord, for wonderful rest. In Jesus' name. Amen.*

2. When we feel overwhelmed by anxious thoughts, what are we to do? As Denise mentioned in the program, we are to take authority by saying, "Devil, you get out of my thoughts. You get out of my emotions. I take authority over you. You have no right to me!" That's shutting the door on the devil. Take a moment and do that now.

3. Jesus is approachable. He is gentle and lowly in heart. Take time to meditate on who He is, and you will find rest.

- "The Lord is my shepherd; I shall not want. He makes me to lie down in green pastures; He leads me beside the still waters. He restores my soul..." (Psalm 23:1-3).

- "The Lord is my light and my salvation; whom shall I fear? The Lord is the strength of my life; of whom shall I be afraid?" (Psalm 27:1).

- "The Lord is my strength and my shield; my heart trusted in Him, and I am helped..." (Psalm 28:7).

LESSON 5

TOPIC

The Secret to Peace

SCRIPTURES

1. **Philippians 4:6-7** — Be anxious for nothing, but in everything by prayer and supplication, with thanksgiving, let your requests be made known to God; and the peace of God, which surpasses all understanding, will guard your hearts and minds through Christ Jesus.

2. **James 4:8** — Draw near to God and He will draw near to you....

3. **2 Chronicles 20:16-21** — "'Tomorrow go down against them. They will surely come up by the Ascent of Ziz, and you will find them at the end of the brook before the Wilderness of Jeruel. You will not need to fight in this battle. Position yourselves, stand still and see the salvation of the Lord, who is with you, O Judah and Jerusalem!' Do not fear or be dismayed; tomorrow go out against them, for the Lord is with you." And Jehoshaphat bowed his head with his face to the ground, and all Judah and the inhabitants of Jerusalem bowed before the Lord, worshiping the Lord. Then the Levites of the children of the Kohathites and of the children of the Korahites stood up to praise the Lord God of Israel with voices loud and high. So they rose early in the morning and went out into the Wilderness of Tekoa; and as they went out, Jehoshaphat stood and said, "Hear me, O Judah and you inhabitants of Jerusalem: Believe in the Lord your God, and you shall be established; believe His prophets, and you shall prosper." And when he had consulted with the people, he appointed those who

should sing to the Lord, and who should praise the beauty of holiness, as they went out before the army and were saying: "Praise the Lord, for His mercy endures forever."

4. **Proverbs 3:5-6** — Trust in the Lord with all your heart, and lean not on your own understanding; in all your ways acknowledge Him, and He shall direct your paths.

5. **Ephesians 3:20** — Now to Him who is able to do exceedingly abundantly above all that we ask or think, according to the power that works in us.

SYNOPSIS

As we bring our cares to the Lord through prayer, supplication, and thanksgiving, He can speak to us and give us instruction that will help us to be filled with His peace and live free from worry. The peace of God acts as an umpire in our hearts, guarding against fear and anxiety, even in the most challenging situations. Just as Jehoshaphat and the people of Israel did when confronted by three massive armies, we can draw near to God in worship, casting our care onto Him and receiving His peace, so He can work supernaturally in our lives to deliver us.

The emphasis of this lesson:

Anything that you are tempted to worry about, you can also pray about! As you draw near to God, you shut out worry and receive His overwhelming peace. This opens the door for you to experience His miraculous power, deliverance, and victory.

Do you realize that you can say goodbye to worry? What a freeing thought! Yes, worries, stress, and anxiety come to all of us. They knock on everyone's door. What matters is whether we open the door or say, "No, you're not coming in." Jesus paid an amazing price so that we might have complete and total peace in our hearts. He paid the price for us to receive His peace, even in the hardest of times. Now, we can experience peace no matter what is going on around us. We can proclaim, "I am not going to be conquered by worry. I'm going to walk in His peace." This is great news!

Say 'No' to Anxious Thoughts

From the biggest care, worry, or problem to the smallest, we are to resist being anxious about anything. Philippians 4:6 and 7 tells us, "Be anxious for nothing, but in everything by prayer and supplication, with thanksgiving, let your requests be made known to God; and the peace of God, which surpasses all understanding, will guard your hearts and minds through Christ Jesus." In the phrase, "be anxious for nothing," the word "nothing" means *the minutest of details, the smallest of details.* God doesn't want us worrying about even the smallest things!

When the apostle Paul wrote these verses in Philippians, he was being held in the most horrible prison. Historians say that he was standing in sewage, and death was all around him. Imagine the stench he endured. Picture the rats that must have crawled in that sewage. Yet he wrote, "Be anxious for nothing." What an example!

If the apostle Paul — by the Holy Spirit — can choose not to worry with such conviction, then we can be sure that God is talking to us through these verses too. He is reaching out right now through His Word and saying to us, "My precious, precious child, don't be anxious for anything." This is God's truth to us.

Choose Prayer, Supplication, and Thanksgiving

Let's take a closer look at this verse. Philippians 4:6 begins by saying, "Be anxious for nothing, but in everything by prayer and supplication...." In everything you face, if you're tempted to worry about it, then you can pray about it. Whatever worries you, talk to God about it. Look up scriptures about it. Declare what God's Word says about it. Supplication is the act of pouring out your heart to God. Tell Him exactly what you want, where you are, and what His Word says about the situation. Say, "God, I'm standing with Your Word on this."

Next, the verse says to make our prayer and supplication "with thanksgiving." Thanksgiving is very important, because as we're pouring out our heart to God, we must continually be thankful for who He is, what He has done in the past, and what He is doing in our life right now. We can be grateful for what He has blessed us with and what we are receiving that others may not have the opportunity to receive. We can rejoice that we can see, talk, and walk. We can sincerely thank God that we have food and a house. Being thankful is so powerful.

When many people pray, they pour out their complaints to the Lord. But then they stop right there, and they don't acknowledge the good things He has done in their life. It's so easy to do that, but it is not what God wants us to do, and it's not where the power is. The power comes when we are tempted to be anxious, but we say no to it. Instead, we pray about it and then thank God for His goodness, magnifying Him for who He is.

Trust the Umpire of Peace in Your Heart

Continuing in Philippians 4:6, it states, "…let your requests be made known to God." God wants to know what our request is. And when we make that request, verse 7 says, "…the peace of God, which surpasses all understanding, will guard your hearts and minds through Christ Jesus."

The peace of God in your heart is like an umpire. Whenever something comes against your heart and mind — something filled with fear, worry, complaints, or anxiety — God's peace stands guard like an umpire. It won't let those negative thoughts and emotions in. It stands up to that worry and says, "No, you are not coming in here."

If you have ever watched hockey, then you have seen how the goalie blocks the puck from entering the goal. When someone sends the hockey puck flying toward the net, the goalie lunges out with his stick to block it. Friend, the peace of God is much greater than an umpire or a hockey goalie. Peace stands up and says, "No, fear — you're not coming in. No, worry — you're not entering in here."

This is how powerful the peace of God is within us! We can listen to His peace, to the umpire within us. We can agree with it and say, "No, I'm not going to take that. I'm going to listen to the peace of God within me."

Side With God and See His Deliverance

What happens when we allow God's powerful peace to infiltrate our lives? James 4:8 says, "Draw near to God and He will draw near to you…." When we choose His peace, we draw near to God, and He draws near to us. In the program, Denise shared a personal experience as an example of how our lives can be transformed as we seek His peace and bring our cares to God with prayer, supplication, and thanksgiving. Below is her story in her own words:

> Many years ago, I was in great distress about something. I wanted a certain situation to change regarding my husband — but it was not changing. So I went to the Lord with my complaints, and the

Holy Spirit spoke to me and said, 'Your husband doesn't need to change. *You* need to change.'

Convicted, I said, 'Lord, how are we going to do that?' I thought of the scripture in James 4:8, which says, 'Draw near to Me, and I will draw near to you.' So I said, 'Lord, I do not know *what* to change. I don't know *how* to change. But I have Your Word, which says that when I draw near to You, then You promise that You will draw near to me.'

Every morning, I rose early and had my eyes in the Word of God. I stayed in the book of Proverbs. But for a long while, I didn't see anything happening. I didn't see my attitude changing.

Then one day I had a thought, and it was as if the Holy Spirit opened my eyes. He said, 'Denise, you have competition in your heart against your husband.'

I said, 'I do? Oh, okay.' I even went and told my husband, 'Rick, the Holy Spirit spoke to me and said I have competition in my heart against you.' I still didn't see anything change. I had just heard the Holy Spirit speak, so I continued to seek Him every morning.

A few days after that, I was seeking the Lord and He drew near to me. He revealed what that competition looked like, the sin of it, the darkness of it, and how it was stealing from me, my relationship with God, and my relationship with my husband. He revealed so much to me. He delivered me in that very moment.

I wept over that revelation for a few days. *But I was completely delivered!* I started out saying, 'Lord, please change my husband.' Then I got deeper than that and said, 'God, I need Your help here.' Finally, God revealed to me, 'Your husband is not your problem. *You* are.' I could have resented that, but I was seeking Him, and I did what His Word said: 'Draw near to God, and He will draw near to you.'

When you draw near to God, He doesn't draw near to you empty-handed. He draws near to you with answers, deliverance, and power for your situation. That's exactly what He did for me that day. He drew near to me with power, answers, and deliverance. And I've never been the same since.

If you want to get rid of anxiety, fear, worry, and complaining, draw close to the One who is never anxious, the One who is never in fear, the One who is completely peaceful. When you draw close to Him, His presence is going to change you.

We Don't Need To Fight the Battle

How can we continually draw near to the Lord, say no to worry, and have His peace in our heart? There is a wonderful example of this in Second Chronicles. The children of Israel were facing an enemy three times larger than themselves. In fact, three different armies had joined together to come against them. It seemed certain that they would be annihilated. But King Jehoshaphat proclaimed a fast, and the people of Israel sought the Lord. Then a prophet of God spoke. Second Chronicles 20:16-21 says:

> "'Tomorrow go down against them. They will surely come up by the Ascent of Ziz, and you will find them at the end of the brook before the Wilderness of Jeruel. You will not need to fight in this battle. Position yourselves, stand still and see the salvation of the Lord, who is with you, O Judah and Jerusalem!" Do not fear or be dismayed; tomorrow go out against them, for the Lord is with you.'
>
> And Jehoshaphat bowed his head with his face to the ground, and all Judah and the inhabitants of Jerusalem bowed before the Lord, worshiping the Lord. Then the Levites of the children of the Kohathites and of the children of the Korahites stood up to praise the Lord God of Israel with voices loud and high.
>
> So they rose early in the morning and went out into the Wilderness of Tekoa; and as they went out, Jehoshaphat stood and said, 'Hear me, O Judah and you inhabitants of Jerusalem: Believe in the Lord your God, and you shall be established; believe His prophets, and you shall prosper.'
>
> And when he had consulted with the people, he appointed those who should sing to the Lord, and who should praise the beauty of holiness, as they went out before the army and were saying: 'Praise the Lord, for His mercy endures forever.'

The children of Israel *worshipped* the Lord. They drew close to the Lord. And when they worshipped the Lord, their assignment from God was to go down to the enemy the next day. But the Word of the Lord said, "You don't need to fight in this battle."

If the people of Israel had been consumed with worry and distrust about what God said, they would never have walked down to their enemy with only one weapon: the praise of God in their mouth. Rather than concentrating on worry and fear, they walked down to the three armies with confidence. As they approached the enemy, they sang, "Praise the Lord, for His mercy endures forever." God's strategy was powerful, and they trusted in the Lord.

The children of Israel made a way for the Lord to do something. Instead of worrying about their problem, holding it in their hands and crying about it, they worshipped the Lord — and they opened space for the supernatural to occur. The next day when they went down and gave praises to the Lord, those three different armies all attacked each other. The spoil was so great that the Israelites collected it for three days!

Open Your Eyes to the Exceeding Abundance of God

How important is it for us to not worry? If we worry, we're closing our eyes to what God wants to do. We hold our care in our hands instead of giving it into His hands. This is like being drunk with worry. Drunk people don't see situations clearly or act completely right because their vision and their personality are affected by the alcohol. Similarly, worry can cause us to perceive things inaccurately. But we can declare that we are not going to worry. We can choose to not let our eyes be blinded anymore, and, instead, see God do great and mighty things.

Proverbs 3:5 and 6 says, "Trust in the Lord with all your heart, and lean not on your own understanding; in all your ways acknowledge Him, and He shall direct your paths." There is a great promise in these verses because if we trust in the Lord, then *we have an open door for Him to direct our paths*. If the children of Israel had worried, refused to believe the prophet, and disobeyed, they would have been killed the next day. But because they trusted in God and worshipped Him, they opened the door for Him to do supernatural things for them.

When we turn away from worry and agree with God's Word, we invite God in to do amazing things. The power we have to say no to worry, anxiety, and complaining opens the door for answers. It makes room for God's power and for the supernatural, just as it did for the children of Israel.

Ephesians 3:20 says, "Now to Him who is able to do exceedingly abundantly above all that we ask or think, according to the power that works in us." If we're worrying, we are not trusting that God is able to do "exceedingly abundantly above all that we ask or think." He has provided us with marvelous things by His Spirit. He's paved the way! Jesus took everything for us so that He could give us everything. As we draw near to Him, we are trusting Him to work in our lives. As we do so, He sets us free from worry so we can walk in His amazing peace and victory!

STUDY QUESTIONS

**Be diligent to present yourself approved to God, a worker
who does not need to be ashamed, rightly dividing the word of truth.
— 2 Timothy 2:15**

1. If you're struggling with anxiety, fear, or worry, draw close to the One who is never anxious, the One who is never in fear, the One who is completely peaceful. What happens when you draw near to God? How will His presence change you? (*Consider* Deuteronomy 4:29; Psalm 139:23-24; Psalm 145:18; Jeremiah 29:13; and James 4:8.)

2. Rather than worrying, pray about the things you are facing. Pour out your heart to God in prayer. What is supplication? What can you expect when you pray? (*Consider* Psalm 119:170; Ephesians 6:18; and Philippians 4:6.)

3. After pouring our heart out to the Lord, it's time for thanksgiving. Why is it important to give thanks after making your requests to God? (*Consider* Psalm 100:4-5; Philippians 4:6; and Colossians 4:2.)

PRACTICAL APPLICATION

**But be doers of the word,
and not hearers only, deceiving yourselves.
— James 1:22**

1. When you draw near to God, He doesn't draw near to you empty-handed. He draws near to you with answers, deliverance, and power

for your situation. Reflect on how the Lord came through for you as you drew near to Him in the midst of a major battle in your life. Write down what God did as you trusted Him in the situation. Meditate on His faithfulness to you in the past and praise Him in advance for His faithfulness to you now and in the future.

2. Power comes when you are tempted to be anxious and worried, but you say no to it. Instead, pray about it and then thank God for His goodness, magnifying Him for who He is. This is how to say goodbye to worry. Whenever you are tempted to worry:

- Talk to God about the situation.

- Look up Scriptures about what you're facing.

- Declare what the truth of God's Word says about your circumstances.

- Say, *God, I'm standing with Your Word on this.*

- By faith, praise God for the answer!

3. As Denise mentioned in the program, as we turn away from worry and trust in the Lord, we open the door for God to do something supernatural. Pray, *Lord, I repent of worrying and I choose to trust You with even the most minute details of my life. I thank You for supernaturally doing exceedingly abundantly above all I could ask or think, and I give You the glory for it. In Jesus' name. Amen.*

A Prayer To Receive Salvation

If you've never received Jesus as your Savior and Lord, now is the time for you to experience the new life Jesus wants to give you! To receive God's gift of salvation that can be obtained through Jesus alone, pray this prayer from your heart:

Jesus, I repent of my sin and receive You as my Savior and Lord. Wash away my sin with Your precious blood and make me completely new. I thank You that my sin is removed, and Satan no longer has any right to lay claim on me. Through Your empowering grace, I faithfully promise that I will serve You as my Lord for the rest of my life.

If you just prayed this prayer of salvation, you are born again! You are a brand-new creation in Christ! Would you please let us know of your decision by going to **renner.org/salvation**? We would love to connect with you and pray for you as you begin your new life in Christ.

Scriptures for further study: John 3:16; John 14:6; Acts 4:12; Ephesians 1:7; Hebrews 10:19,20; 1 Peter 1:18,19; Romans 10:9,10; Colossians 1:13; 2 Corinthians 5:17; Romans 6:4; 1 Peter 1:3

Notes

CLAIM YOUR FREE RESOURCE!

As a way of introducing you further to the teaching ministry of Rick Renner, we would like to send you FREE of charge his teaching, "How To Receive a Miraculous Touch From God" on CD or as an MP3 download.

In His earthly ministry, Jesus commonly healed *all* who were sick of *all* their diseases. In this profound message, learn about the manifold dimensions of Christ's wisdom, goodness, power, and love toward all humanity who came to Him in faith with their needs.

☑ **YES, I want to receive Rick Renner's monthly teaching letter!**

Simply scan the QR code to claim this resource or go to:
renner.org/claim-your-free-offer

Connect WITH US!

Dear Friend,

If you enjoyed this study guide and believe others would benefit from reading it, please leave a review on Amazon and recommend it to others — or *consider sharing a copy with a friend or loved one!*

There is a great need for *"teaching you can trust"* among God's people.

Your friends in Christ and for His Gospel,

Dirk & Denise Kramer